Homemade Cakes

By Cameron Macintosh

My nan bakes the best homemade birthday cakes.

She makes each cake with a theme.

When I was two,
Nan made a tadpole cake.

Nan said I was the tadpole.
Mum, Nan and Holt were the frogs!

When I turned five,
Nan made lots of cupcakes
with rosebuds on top.

Then Nan helped me bake extra cupcakes to take to school.

I gave some to my schoolmates.

When I turned six,
I told Nan I wanted a wildlife cake.

She made a wildcat cake
by mistake.

A wildcat is still wildlife,
I suppose!

Nan made a reptile cake
for my seventh birthday.

It was so lifelike!

When I turned eight,
Nan made birthday pancakes.

I helped make them!

We gave them an upgrade
from plain pancakes
to canine pancakes!

Nan made a music cake
when I turned nine!

That's because I play trombone
in my school band.

Nan said that when I am ten,
I'll be a big kid.

Ten is a "milestone".

I would like a sport cake
that includes an athlete
that wins the prize!

FINISH

What homemade cake should Nan make next?

I can't choose!

CHECKING FOR MEANING

1. What sort of cake did Nan make when the narrator turned seven? *(Literal)*
2. How old will the narrator be on her next birthday? *(Literal)*
3. Why do you think Nan made a mistake with the narrator's sixth birthday? *(Inferential)*
4. Which cake do you think has the best theme? Why? *(Evaluative)*

EXTENDING VOCABULARY

homemade	How many syllables are in the word *homemade*? What two smaller words make up the word *homemade*? How do these smaller words help you understand the meaning of the whole word?
canine	What is a canine? What is another word the narrator could have used instead of *canine*?
milestone	What is a milestone? Why is turning ten years old a milestone?

MOVING BEYOND THE TEXT

1. What theme would you choose for a cake for a birthday or other special occasion? Why?
2. What are some other things that can be homemade?
3. Cakes are a treat food. What kinds of healthy foods should you eat regularly? What is your favourite fruit or vegetable?
4. What special occasions do you like to celebrate?

TIME TO WRITE

Imagine you are making your own special cake with a theme. Write about the theme you have chosen, and about how you would decorate your cake.